Mother's

EASY ANSWERS

TO LIFE'S DIFFICULT QUESTIONS

Mother's EASY ANSWERS
TO LIFE'S DIFFICULT QUESTIONS

HEATH & MOLLIE HARMISON

PLAIN SIGHT PUBLISHING
AN IMPRINT OF CEDAR FORT, INC.
SPRINGVILLE, UT

ISBN 13: 978-1-4621-4219-4

Published by Plain Sight Publishing, an imprint of Cedar Fort, Inc.
2373 W. 700 S., Springville, UT 84663
Distributed by Cedar Fort, Inc., www.cedarfort.com

Library of Congress Control Number: 2022930830

Cover design by Shawnda T. Craig
Interior layout and designs by Shawnda T. Craig & Courtney Proby
Cover design © 2022 Cedar Fort, Inc.

Printed in the United States of America

10 9 8 7 6 5 4 3 2 1

Printed on acid-free paper

I dedicate this book to the most fulfilling and least validated job on the planet—motherhood! And to every mom out there—you freaking matter! Without you, there'd be a whole bunch of serial killers!

So good job, we've got this! I see you!

—Mollie

Do I have to go to yoga today?

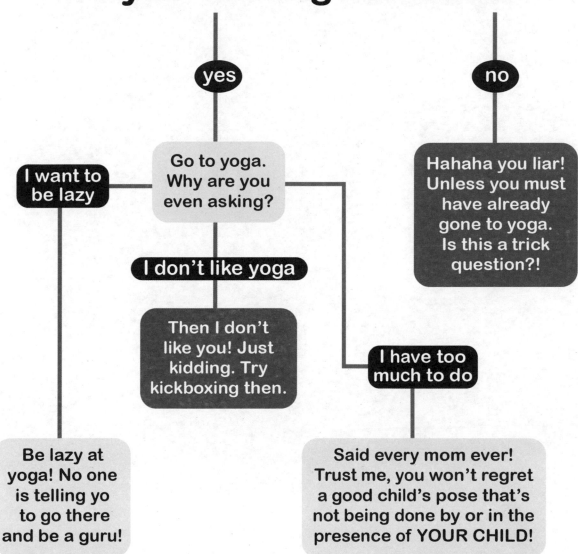

Probably because you need
more blubber in your diet.
Fat is nature's blanket.
You might have a heart
attack, but you'll be warm.

Is it family game night?

Do you like playing games?

Yes

No → Play "Hide and Seek." When they all go hide, go to your room, lock the door, and listen to your favorite True Crime podcast.

Do you have an unhealthy competitive spirit?

No → Sounds like a fun night! Let the games begin!

Yes → Maybe you should just throw on a movie so you don't berate your child by calling them a loser when you win.

Am i on my phone too much?

Do you use it for more than making phone calls?

Yes!!!!

Does Tiktok, Instagram, Facebook, Twitter, and SnapChat count?

No

That's a big fat yes! However, you are reading a book right now, so give yourself a break.

What?! Are you living under a rock? Although, maybe you're on to something. Kudos for the self control...or fear of the outside world.

You have a problem. Go spend some time in the woods.

DO I NEED to shave MY LEGS?

ARE YOU A
hippie? — yes

no

Are you single?

yes

no

yes — Keep the hair, but if you don't have many friends, then focus on your smell. Organic deodorant doesn't work!

no — Trust me, your person doesn't want your forest of hair rubbing against them in the middle of the night!

yes — It's probably because you look like a wookie . . . shave!

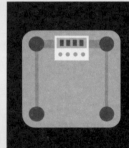

WORKOUT

OR

BRUNCH?

MENU

DID YOU WORK OUT YESTERDAY?

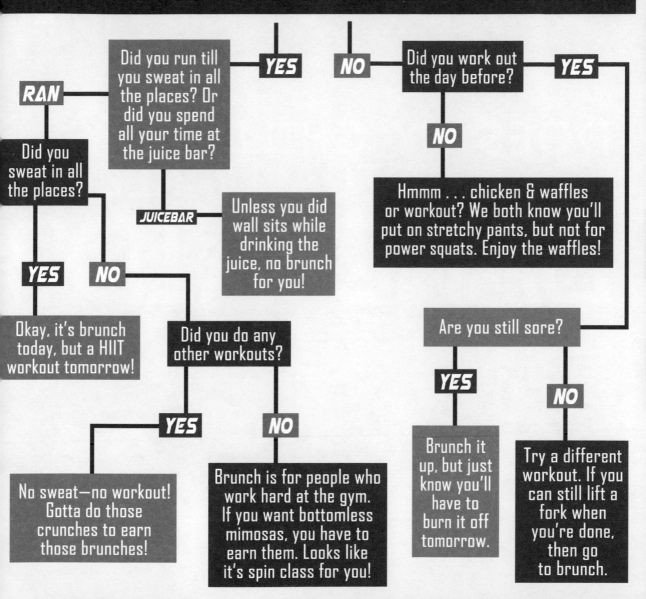

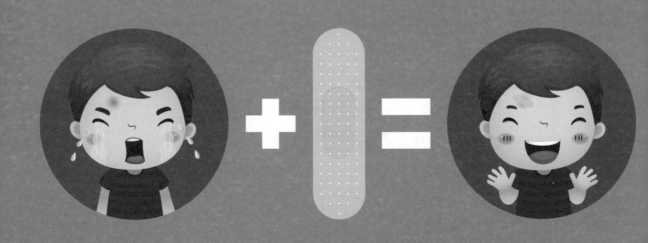

DOES MY CHILD ACTUALLY NEED A BAND-AID?

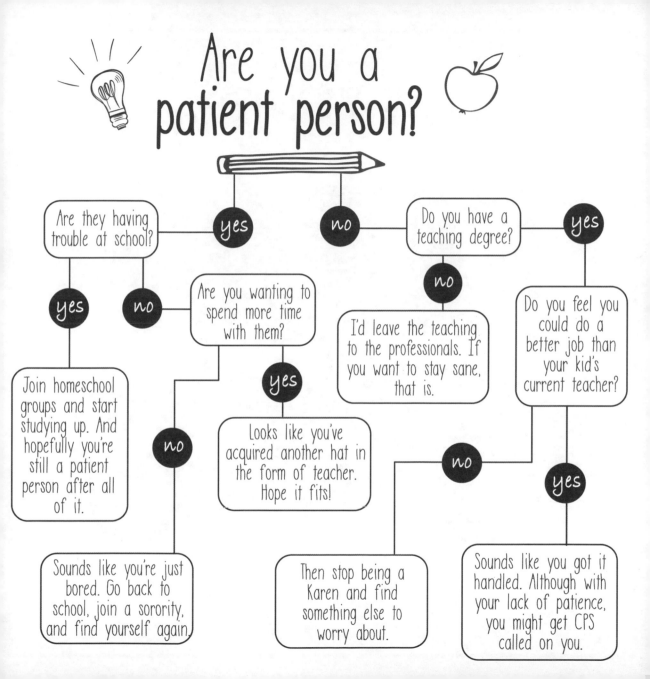

SHOULD WE LIVE ON A FARM?

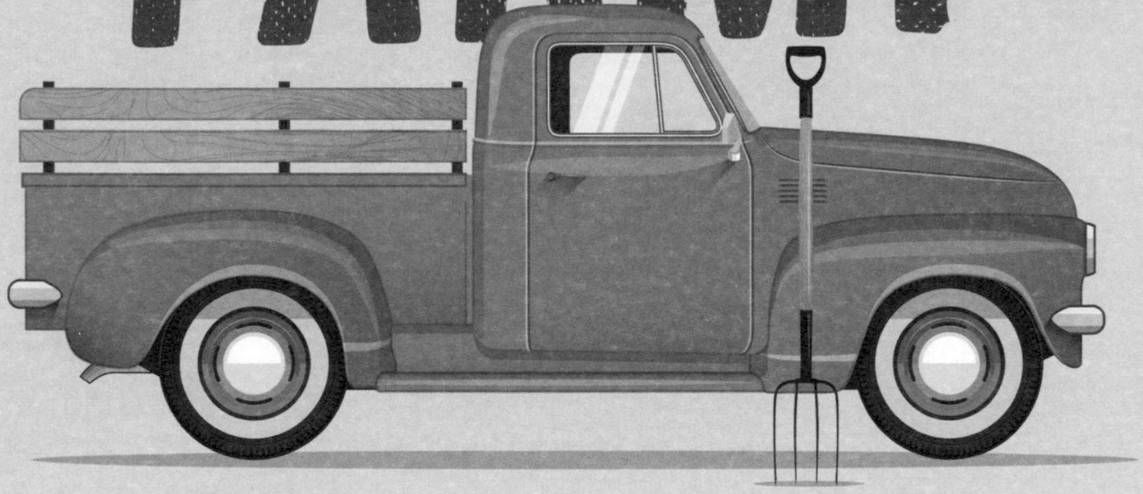

ALL FRESH NATURAL ORGANIC FOOD

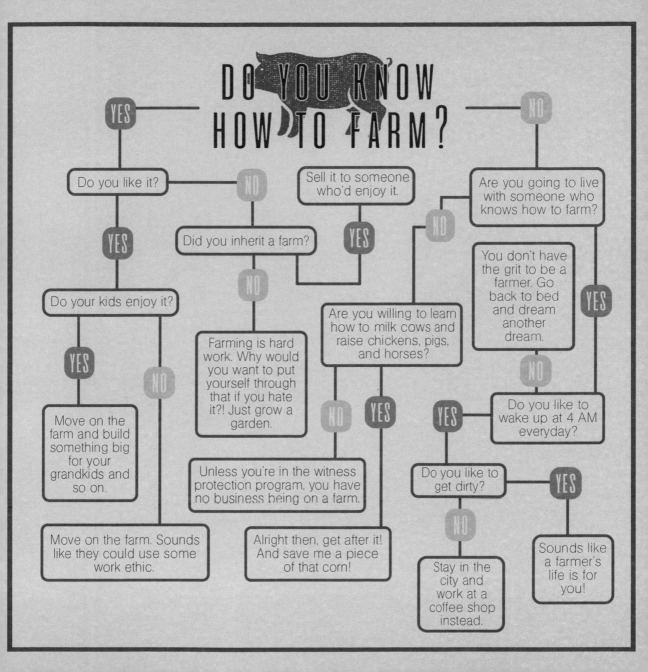

Are you sprouting hairs in places you never have before?

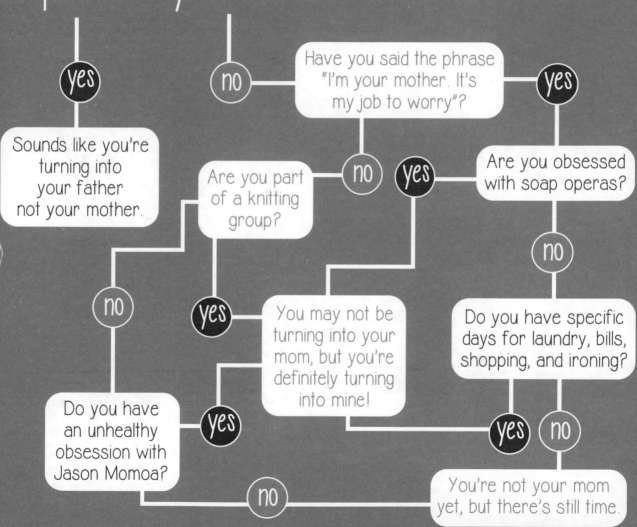

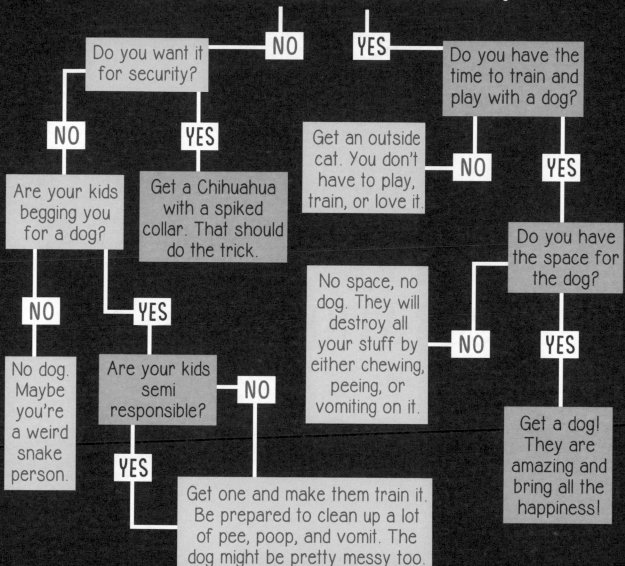

SHOULD I TAKE MY CHRISTMAS DECORATIONS DOWN?

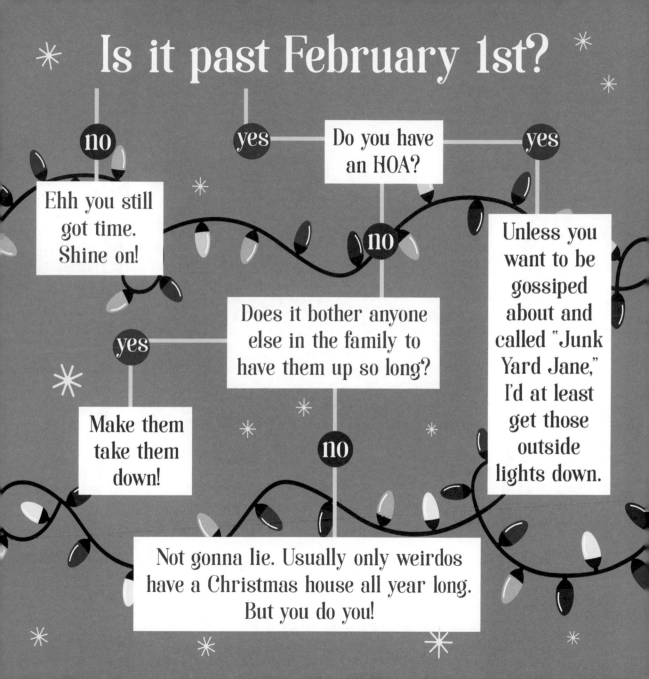

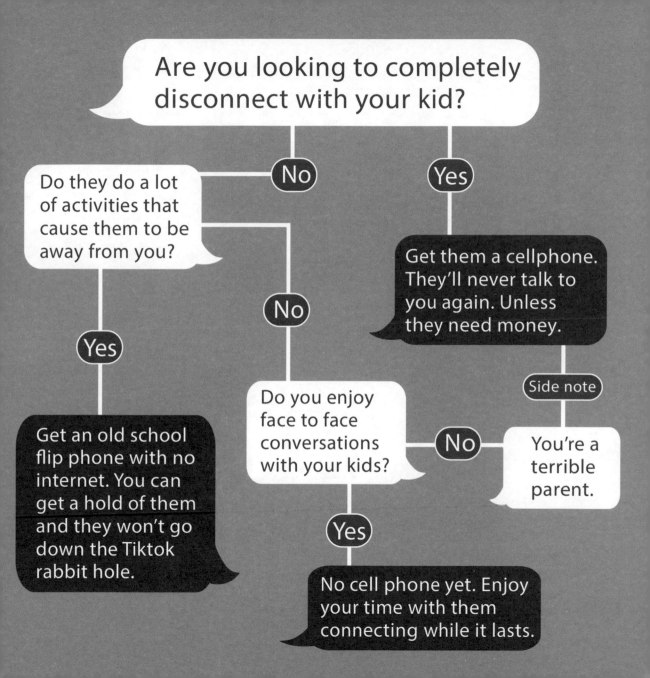

Does my kid NEED to wear pants?

Is your child under 10?

no → **yes** → Are they potty training?

Yes, your child needs to wear pants! Unless you both want to be arrested.

Is it hot outside?

no → **yes** → Save yourself the trouble and let them go willy nilly. Just don't let them pee on an electric fence.

Do you own a trampoline?

yes → **no** → Do they simply refuse to wear pants?

yes → **no** → No trampoline?! Well, there's your first problem. That's the world's best babysitter!

no → **yes**

Put a sprinkler under that bad boy and let them go wild! They have fun and you don't have to bathe them tonight.

Find their favorite pair. They may just prefer leopard print or rainbow pants, but at least they are wearing pants.

Career choices start early. Get those pants on!

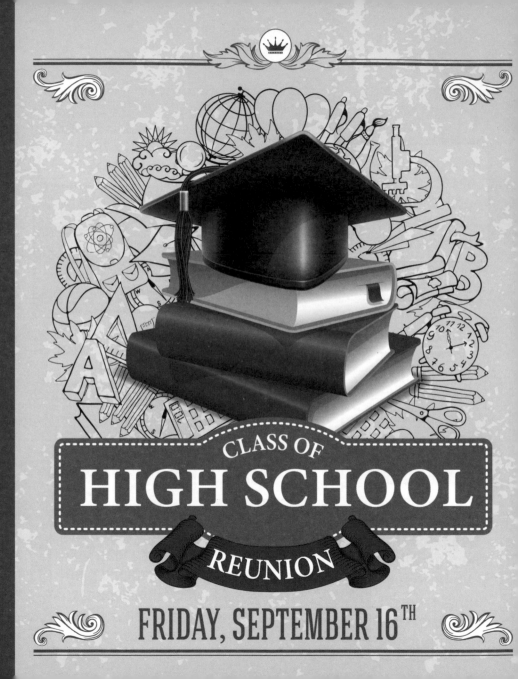

SHOULD I GO TO MY HIGH SCHOOL REUNION?

CLASS OF

HIGH SCHOOL

REUNION

FRIDAY, SEPTEMBER 16TH

DO YOU LOOK BETTER THAN YOU DID IN HIGH SCHOOL?

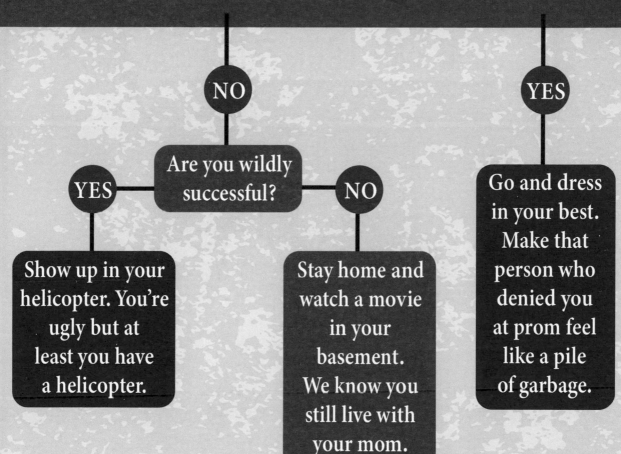

NO

YES

Are you wildly successful?

YES

NO

Show up in your helicopter. You're ugly but at least you have a helicopter.

Stay home and watch a movie in your basement. We know you still live with your mom.

Go and dress in your best. Make that person who denied you at prom feel like a pile of garbage.

SHOULD I

GET A TATTOO?

WILL IT BE ON YOUR FACE?

no
↓

yes
↓

GO FOR IT! If it's text make sure it's spelled correctly. You don't want to have any REGERTS.

It sounds like you're prone to bad decisions. Maybe you should rethink this one.

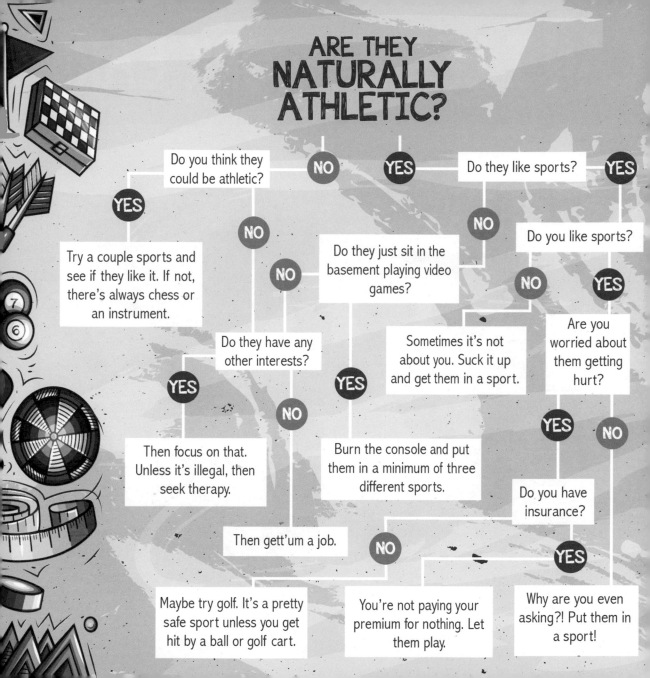

IS YOUR BOSS STILL THERE?

ERROR

YES → Do you have big plans?

NO → Will there be unfavorable consequences to you leaving?

I AM THE BOSS → Is this your away-from-home job, or your full-time parent job?

Do you have big plans?
- **YES** → If these "big plans" weren't planned with notice, they probably aren't big enough. No emergency, no leaving work early.
- **NO** → If you want to keep your job, you can't blow it off for Netflix. Stay at work!

Will there be unfavorable consequences to you leaving?
- **YES** → Is it worth the risk?
  - **YES** → Why are you still debating. You obviously have something better to do.
- **NO** → Why are you still debating. You obviously have something better to do.

Is this your away-from-home job, or your full-time parent job?

FUL- TIME PARENT
What's your rush to go from one job to the next? I'd say go to the one with better company and less demands.

AWAY FROM HOME
Who do you think you're fooling? You're not the boss. But you can schedule your own sick day every once in a while and do nothing. Do it!

WARNING!

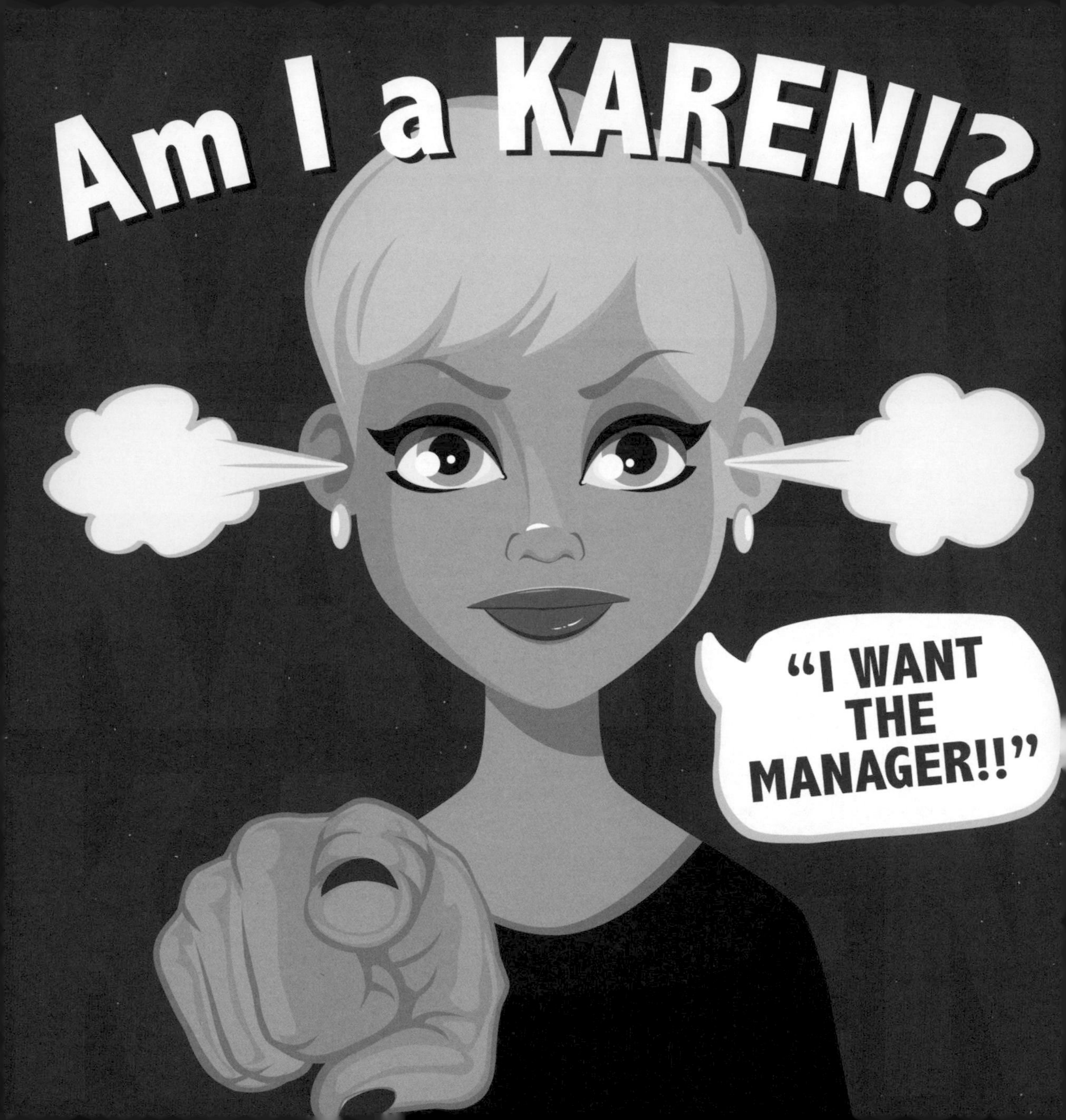
Am I a KAREN!?
"I WANT THE MANAGER!!"

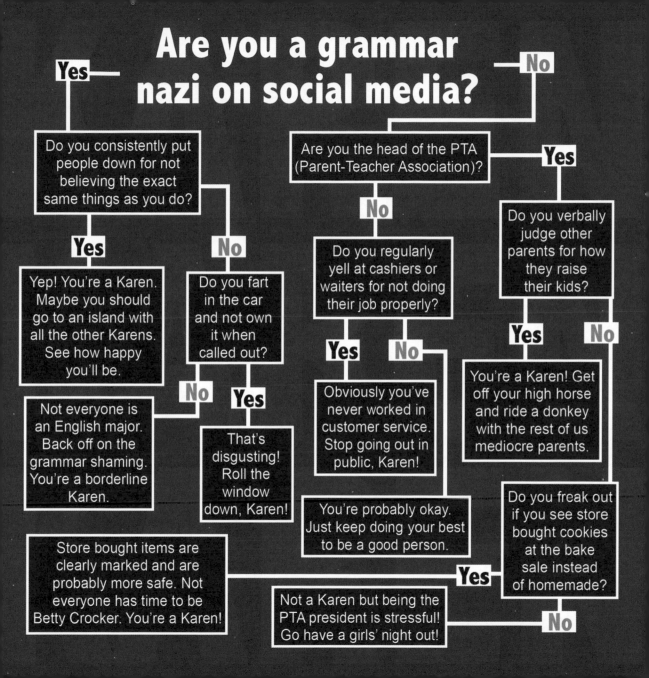

SHOULD I FIRE MY NANNY?

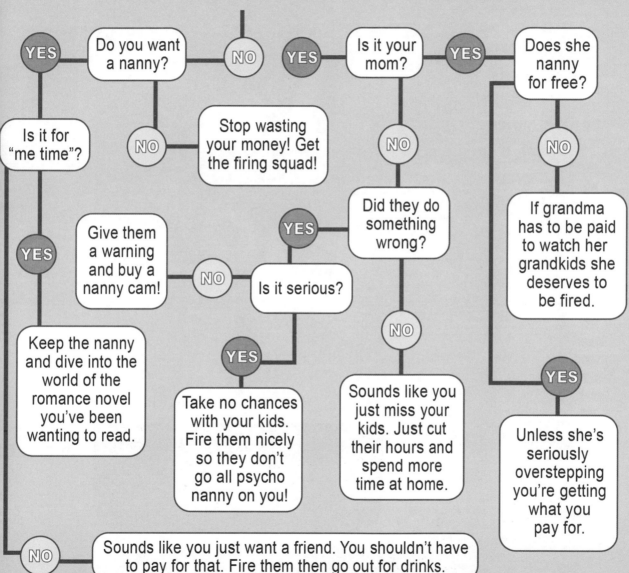

Should I download TikTok?

Are you bored?

NO

Oh so you already have TikTok then.

YES Can you Dance?

NO

YES

Then TikTok isn't for you. Amateur dancing at best.

NO

It's fine you don't have to make videos. But watching them will suck you into a dark abyss.

Do you sing, do killer makeup, impressions, tell sappy stories, or just act like an idiot?

YES Then you're perfect for TikTok!

Most likely, but do you have time for a shower?

no

yes

Sponge bath time. Wash the parts & call it good. Make time for a shower though, seriously.

Shower! Who knows when you'll have time for another one!

I forgot my

Anniversary

What do I do?

Is this the first time you've forgotten?

Did your spouse forget?

no

yes

Did your spouse forget?

yes

no

You know that thing they always want you to do but you don't want to? Do it!!

no

yes

Call your lawyer.

Celebrate with some marriage counseling. Sounds like you both need it.

Do they know you forgot?

no

You need to think fast and move quick! Put on something that will make them drool! Then go out and do their favorite thing!

yes

Welcome to the dog house. Get them something special. Expect the cold shoulder. Do better next year . . . if you make it.

IS IT A LEGGINGS & messybun KIND of DAY? ♡

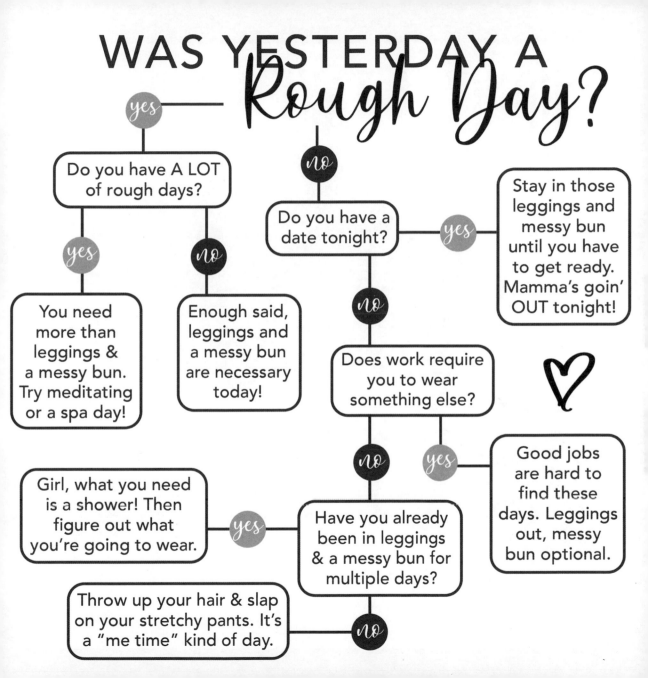

ARE YOU ANGRY AND/OR NEEDING TO LET OUT SOME AGGRESSION?

NO

YES! ALL THE TIME!

DEFINITELY! In fact, pair it with some yoga before you hurt someone.

SOMETIMES

Do you sit at a desk or watch daytime TV with Cheeto-stained fingers?

YES

Looking for a great workout?

NO

Are you already active in other types of exercise?

Do you have coworkers near you or children still living at home?

YES

SOMETIMES

Try kickboxing. Bonus, you'll meet equally somewhat-off-their-rocker individuals that you can hang out with. At least they don't do CrossFit.

YES **NO**

Try kickboxing. It's cheaper than therapy, and you, my friend, need some!

YES **NO**

You have anger. Let it out kickboxing instead of on your idiot coworker Terry—who may also be your son.

Wow! It looks like you need more consistency than "sometimes." Get the ALL ACCESS membership today!

For a change try kickboxing. Or plan a girl's trip. Did someone say half marathon?

Sometimes kids not living with you are more stressful. Get your kicks and boxing on!

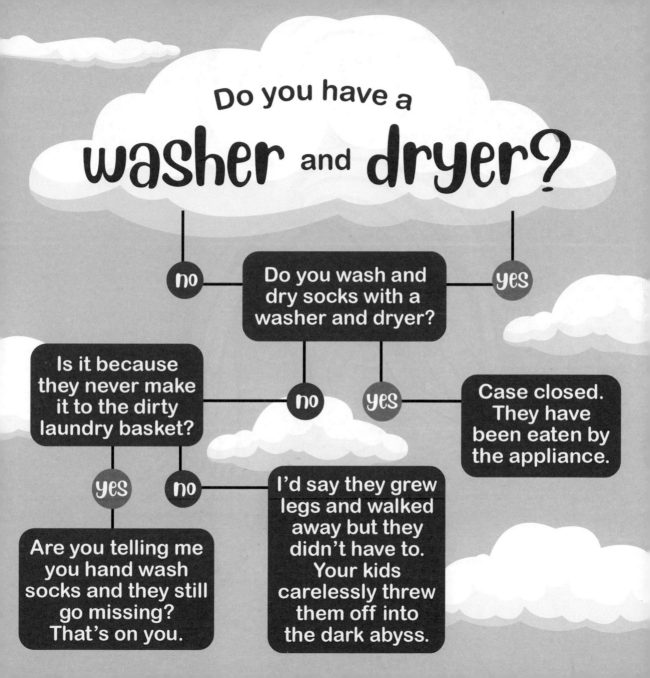

SHOULD I CALL MY EX?
NO! NEVER CALL YOUR EX!
THEY ARE YOUR EX FOR A REASON!

CAN I SKIP
the Family
Reunion
THIS YEAR?

Did you go last year?

yes

Is the reunion this year going camping or a cruise?

Camping

Cruise

GO.

Do you like camping?

yes — Go. Maybe it'll unzombify the kids.

no — Skip it. No plumbing is a no-no.

no

Did you go the year before?

yes — Go. One year off, one year on.

no

The year before that?

yes — Maybe they won't notice? Skip it.

no

Go. They might think you're dead.

Did anyone hear it?

No

Sit back and watch your butt demon possess all the people around you.

Yes

Blame it on the closest old person and repent later.

Am I a
CONSPIRACY THEORIST?

ARE YOU ALWAYS TALKING ABOUT ANY OF THE THINGS LISTED BELOW?

- The moon landing being fake
- Big foot is real
- The earth being hollow
- Prince Charles is a vampire
- The Titanic didn't sink
- 5G causes cancer
- Bill Gates . . . anything Bill Gates
- The Loch Ness monster lives in Scotland
- The abominal snowman lives in Asia

- Who killed JFK
- The earth being flat
- Aliens
- The moon isn't real
- Zombies are real
- We're being chipped

No

Yes

You're not a conspiracy theorist. At least not a good one.

You are, and people are talking. Congrats! Get your tin foil hat on. You're late for your online group nut job meeting.

If you have to ask, they probably are. Have fun with it. We're all raising liars now and then.

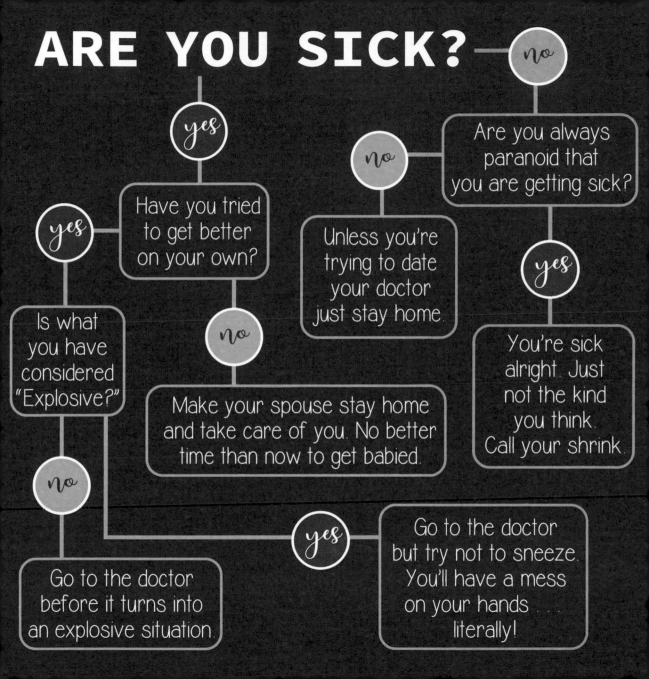

where are all the forks?

SHOULD I WAX MY *Eyebrows?*

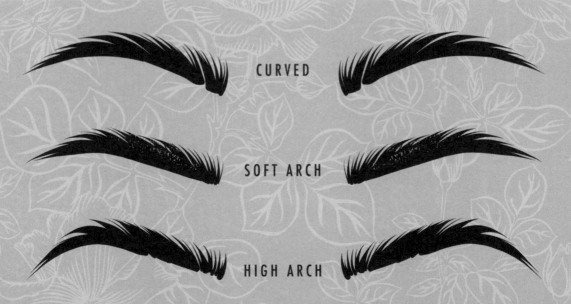

CURVED

SOFT ARCH

HIGH ARCH

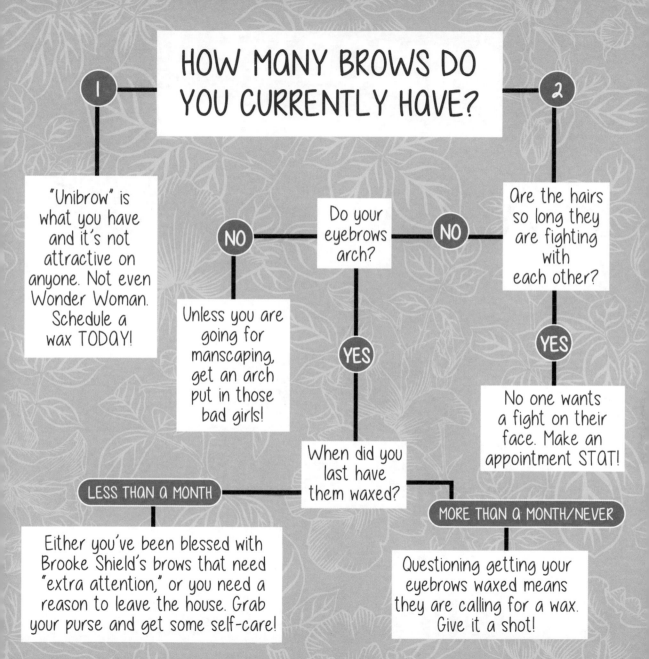

ARE YOU IN A PUBLIC PLACE?

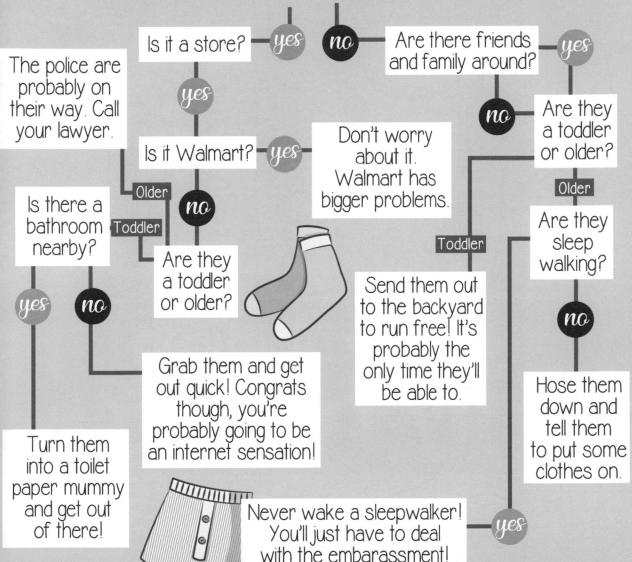

Is it a store? **yes** — **no** — Are there friends and family around? — **yes**

The police are probably on their way. Call your lawyer.

yes

Is it Walmart? **yes** Don't worry about it. Walmart has bigger problems.

no

Are they a toddler or older? — **no**

Older

Are they sleep walking?

Is there a bathroom nearby?

Older

Toddler

Are they a toddler or older?

yes **no**

no

Toddler

Send them out to the backyard to run free! It's probably the only time they'll be able to.

Grab them and get out quick! Congrats though, you're probably going to be an internet sensation!

Turn them into a toilet paper mummy and get out of there!

Hose them down and tell them to put some clothes on.

Never wake a sleepwalker! You'll just have to deal with the embarassment!

yes

Should I clean my house?

Is it already clean?

Are you avoiding doing something else?

yes → yes

no

When was the last time it was cleaned?

no

Who knows?

Is the "something else" important?

Do you get anxiety from one little thing being out of place?

Not really

Do your "something else." Your house is clean, lady!

yes

Yesterday

Do you have some kind of chore chart?

yes

You sound a bit OCD. Take a nap or call a doctor.

How old are your kids/kid?

no

yes

Teenagers

Put your big girl pants on and stop using your domestic career of "being a mom" as an excuse!

Toddlers/Preteen

Your house can't be too bad then. Their room on the other hand . . .

I'd make one and stick to it before your house is more full of rodents than children.

Newborn

Your house is probably fine. You are not. Take a nap.

They've easily already destroyed your house. Get all hands on deck and clean it!

The chore chart obviously isn't working. Maybe it's time to hire a cleaning person.

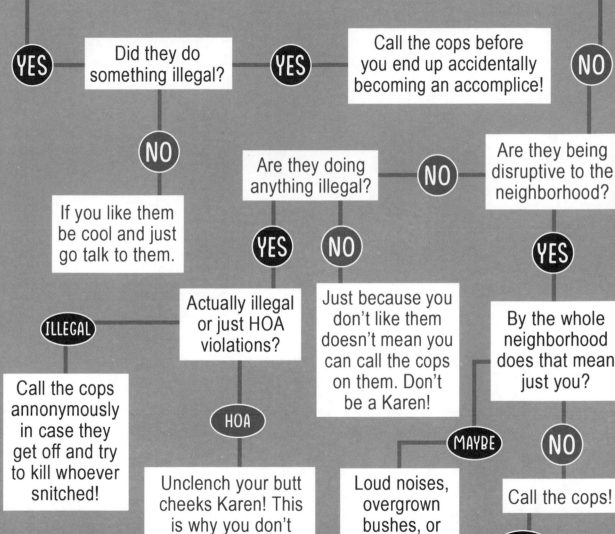

SHOULD I GO SKYDIVING?

ARE YOU AFRAID OF HEIGHTS?

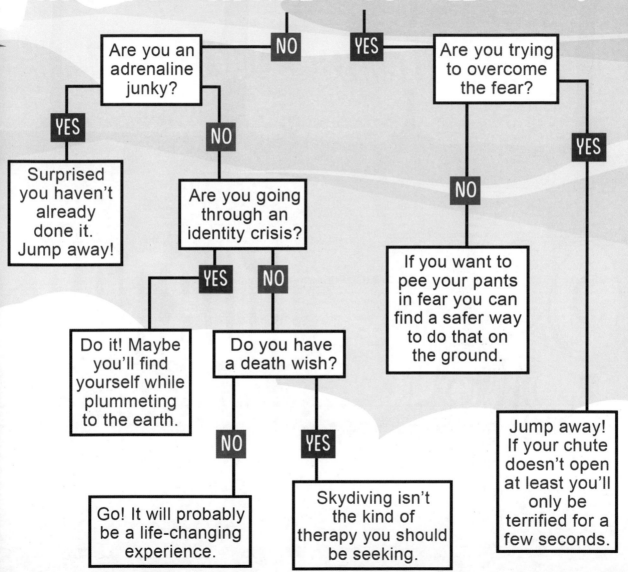

Should we watch a HORROR MOVIE?

Do you like horror movies?

Does your spouse like them? — yes

no — **Have you had trouble going to the bathroom?**

yes

A couple that's scared together stays together. Unless your husband screams higher than you. It's your call.

no

Watch it! There's nothing better than watching your spouse scream like a little girl!

Do you have the hiccups? — no

no

Compromise and watch the Halloween episodes of sitcoms.

yes

Put on an adult diaper and watch the scariest movie you can think of and just let it happen.

yes

No scary movie needed. Drink a glass of water upside down in a haunted house.

IS THE BOY BAND FROM YOUR TEENAGE YEARS?

Yes

BACKSTREET BOYS, NSYNC, 98 DEGREES, AND NEW KIDS ON THE BLOCK ARE OK!
BUT NO HANSEN. MMMBOP THEM OFF THE LIST.

No

RAAR! THAT'S ALL I CAN SAY ABOUT THAT YA COUGAR!

Is my makeup on point?

EYEBROW

MAKEUP
POWDER PUFF

SHADER

LIPSTICK

BROWBRUSH
& COMB

SHADER

BROWBRUSH
& COMB

Do you love it?

no — **yes**

no → Do you contour? → *What's that?* → Watch a YouTube video. That's a start.

yes (from Do you love it? yes) → Do other people give you compliments?

Do you contour? → **yes** ↓

Does it blend with your skintone? → **no** → Visit a makeup counter or a pro artist. No one wants orange skin!

Do other people give you compliments? → **yes** / **no**

yes → Do you feel up to speed on the latest makeup trends?

no (compliments) → Just because you love it doesn't mean it's working. But if you're happy, FORGET EM!

Does it blend with your skintone? → **yes** ↓

Do you do the same makeup every day? → **no** → You need inspiration. Host a makeup night with friends or go to a dragshow! You'll see all sorts of different looks there.

Do you feel up to speed on the latest makeup trends? → **yes** / **no**

yes ↓

Do you do the same makeup every day? → **yes** ↓

Mix it up. Throw on a different eyeshadow. Maybe blue? The 90s are back!

yes → Sounds like you need to share your knowledge and beauty tips with those less fortunate.

no → Who is?! You're fine. If you're loving it, it's on point!

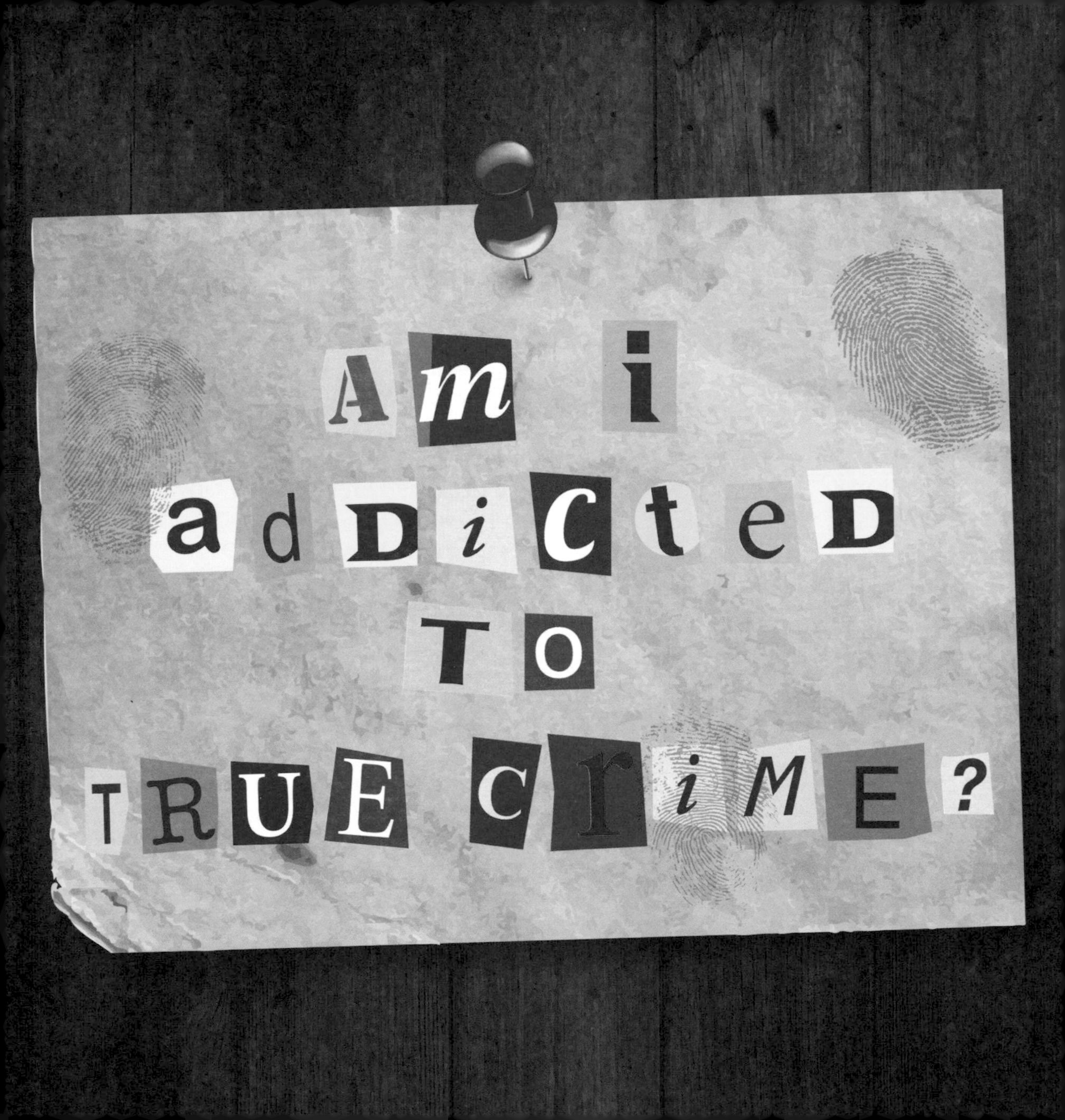
Am I addicted to TRUE CRiME?

Do you watch, read, or listen to something True Crime related everyday?

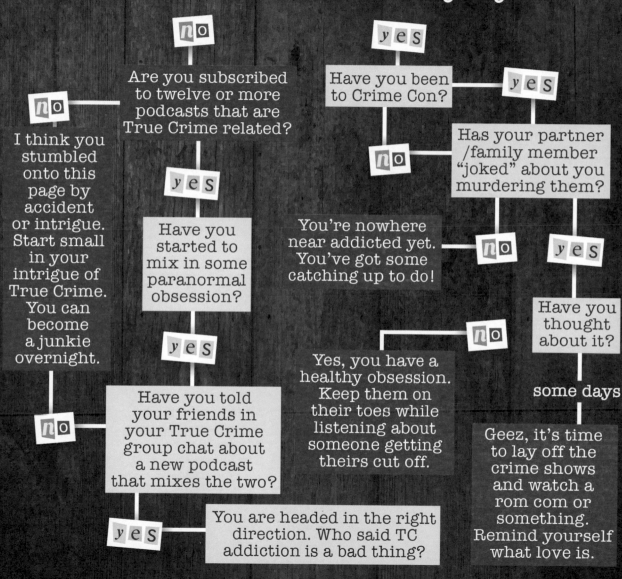

no

Are you subscribed to twelve or more podcasts that are True Crime related?

no

I think you stumbled onto this page by accident or intrigue. Start small in your intrigue of True Crime. You can become a junkie overnight.

yes

Have you started to mix in some paranormal obsession?

yes

Have you told your friends in your True Crime group chat about a new podcast that mixes the two?

no

yes

You are headed in the right direction. Who said TC addiction is a bad thing?

yes

Have you been to Crime Con?

no

You're nowhere near addicted yet. You've got some catching up to do!

Yes, you have a healthy obsession. Keep them on their toes while listening about someone getting theirs cut off.

yes

Has your partner /family member "joked" about you murdering them?

no

yes

Have you thought about it?

no

some days

Geez, it's time to lay off the crime shows and watch a rom com or something. Remind yourself what love is.

SHOULD I PLANT A GARDEN?

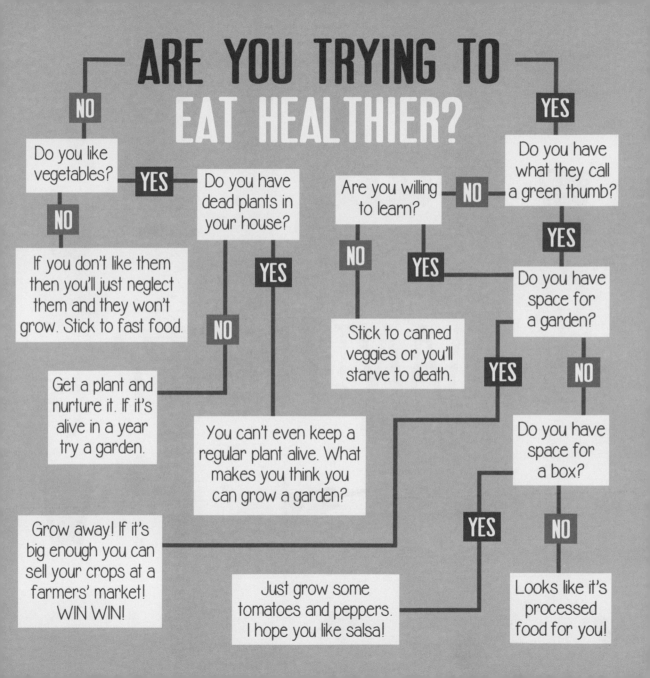

DO YOU WAKE UP WITH SHREDDED BED SHEETS?

Yes

Do your hands look as if you could be the next Wolverine?

No

Do they look like potato chips in shape and color?

No

Unless you want to be pampered there's no need.

Yes

You don't need a nail salon. You need a podiatrist. Get to the doctor!

Yes

Are you trying to break a world's record for longest nails?

No

Get into a nail salon stat!

Yes

Make your dreams come true! Let 'em grow!

No

Have you accidentally drawn blood from your significant other in the middle of the night ?

Yes

Get those puppies shaved down before you become a story on a true crime podcast!

No

Did you run a marathon and your toenails fell off and grew back weird?

No

You probably don't need it, but you can always pamper yourself.

Yes

You need this! Either that or never wear sandals.

SHOULD I TAKE MY KIDS TO THE PARK?

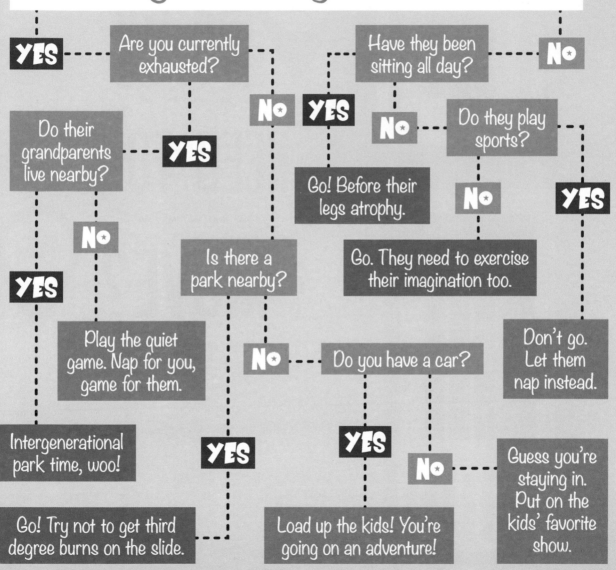

DO WE NEED TO MOVE?

DO YOU LIKE YOUR CURRENT RESIDENCE?

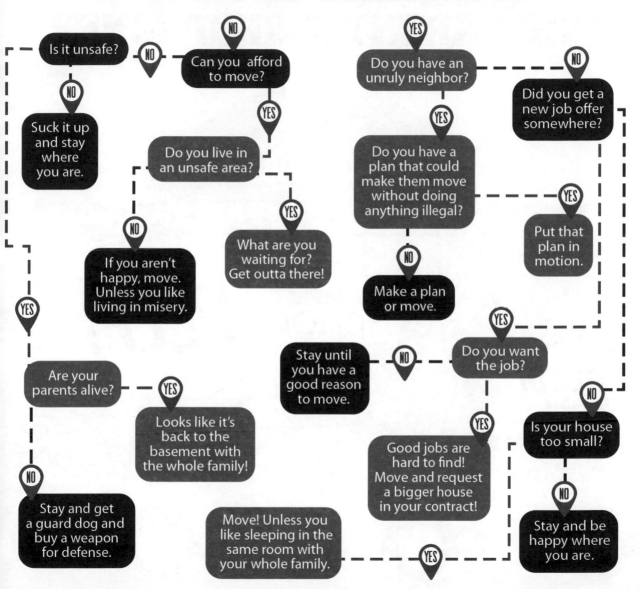

ARE YOU RUNNING LATE?

NO — **YES**

NO branch

NO ← Are you just bored?

YES (from "Are you just bored?")
Throw on some tunes and jam out. Be the cool car in school.

Chick has it coming. Cut the line, make eye contact, and give her the "I'm watching you" sign.

Is your kid embarassed of you?

NO (to "Is your kid embarassed of you?")

NO (down)
Are you just wanting to piss off the parent pickup guard? AKA Meredith?

YES →
Pull your hair up and throw on a cute cardigan next time. School is hard enough on these kids!

YES (from "Are you just wanting to piss off...")

NO (down)
Sounds like you're just looking to cause trouble. Plan a ladies' night for that and leave parent pickup out of it.

Make your kid walk from where you're parked. It'll give them a mediocre "I walked to school" story for their own kids.

YES branch

Late because you woke up late or something beyond your control?

WOKE UP LATE
You deserve to be late. Be more responsible!

BEYOND MY CONTROL
Do they have a parent pickup guard on duty?

YES (down) — **NO**

Is she a Karen? Or worse, a Meredith?

NO ← **YES** (down)

Cash in the "I've got bigger problems" card. Just don't make eye contact when you cut the line.

All the more reason to do it! Lead by example in pissing off the Merediths of the world.

Should I take my kids to Disneyland?

Do your kids like roller coasters?

Yes

No

Are they into classic Disney characters, Marvel superheroes, or Star Wars?

Don't waste your money. Take them to the McDonald's Playland instead.

Are they obsessed with all things Disney?

Yes

No

Yes

Do you enjoy waiting in lines while sweating in all the crevices of your body?

Don't waste your money. Try Six Flags or Universal Studios.

No

Is it worth taking out a second mortgage for them to hang out with a bunch of fake versions of Disney characters?

No

Yes

Yes

Do you care enough about your kids' happiness to put yourself through that?

Well then the Magical World of Disney is for you! Enjoy the rides and $20 hotdogs.

Sounds like you have an unhealthy obsession with Disney. Have fun!

No

Yes

No

Try Vegas. They have them too. . . kind of. And it's cheaper, unless you have a gambling problem.

Good luck and wear a diaper. You'll probably need it waiting in those lines.

Put on their favorite Disney movie at home. That should be good enough.

Is my wardrobe outdated?

have you bought

anything brand new

in the last 1-5 years?

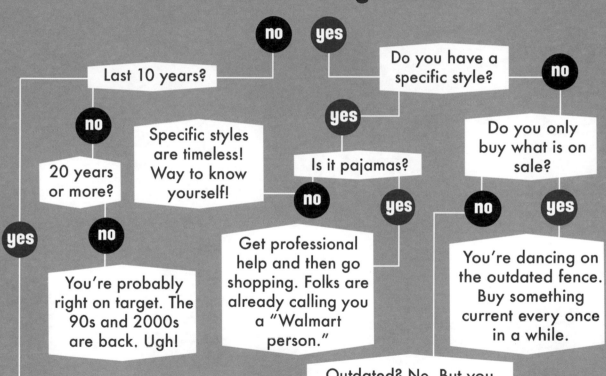

no **yes**

Do you have a specific style? → **no**

Last 10 years?

no

20 years or more?

Specific styles are timeless! Way to know yourself!

Is it pajamas?

Do you only buy what is on sale?

yes **no**

no **yes**

no **yes**

You're probably right on target. The 90s and 2000s are back. Ugh!

Get professional help and then go shopping. Folks are already calling you a "Walmart person."

You're dancing on the outdated fence. Buy something current every once in a while.

You don't eat bread after its expiration date. Why are you wearing all the same old clothes? Outdated, YES.

Outdated? No. But you could use some fashion 411 on finding your own style. Binge watch some makeover shows!

WHAT IS THAT SMELL?

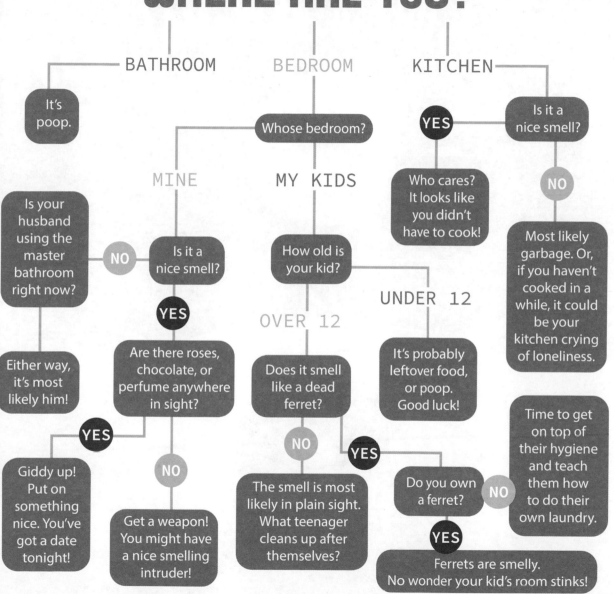

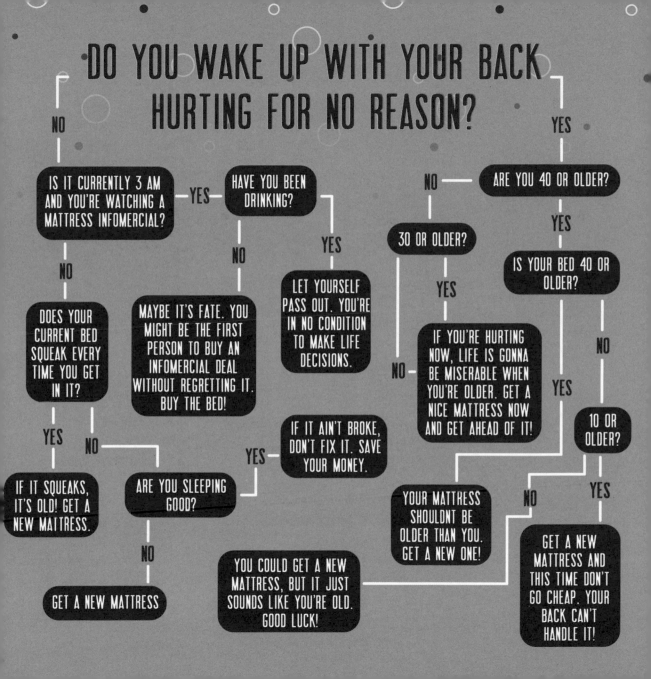

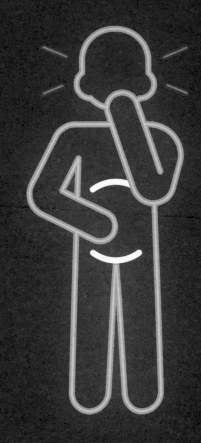

WHY IS MY
STOMACH UPSET?

Are you anxious about something?

NO → **Did you eat today?**

NO → Well duh, your stomach is screaming at you like a hungry child to feed it!

YES → **Did you eat out or at home?**

ATE OUT → **Do you have a food allergy?**

NO → It could be food poisoning. Or you ate too much. Either way avoid that place for a while.

YES → **Were you specific in your ordering to leave out said allergen?**

NO → That's on you, my friend. Find your EpiPen and make better choices!

YES → They probably still put it in there. Don't eat there again.

ATE AT HOME → **Could someone in your house be poisoning you?**

YES → Geez!! That was a joke! Get help now!

NO → **Did you eat too much today?**

NO → Probably expired food. It Looks like you're doing the poisoning. Throw it out!

YES → Stop overeating! Take some Tums and do better tomorrow.

YES → **Is it something important?**

NO → Put on your pjs, take a melatonin, and RELAX! The world is not ending today.

YES → Your stomach is basically another brain. Listen to it and not just the gurgling.

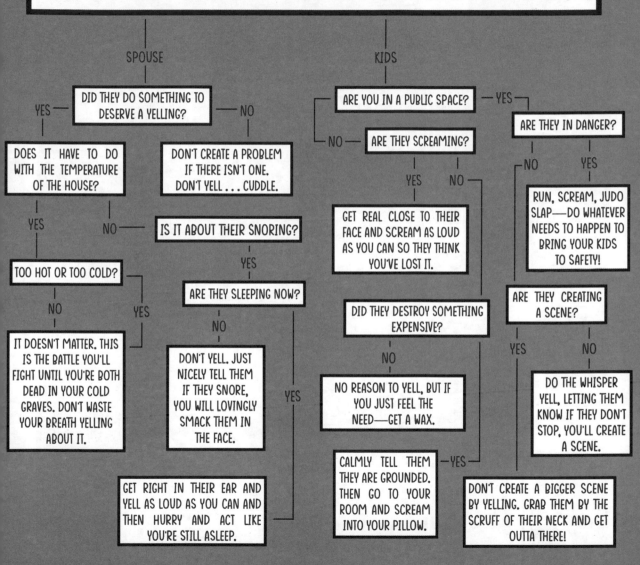

Should I take
my kids to
a concert?

LORUM PRESENTS
LIVE IN CONCERT

AFTER SHOW INCLUDED

GATE 02 ROW 08 SEAT 67

ADMISSION NO. 4015 5620 001

LORUM PRESENTS
LIVE IN CONCERT
GATE 02 ROW 08 SEAT 67
LORUM PRESENTS
RT

live music

Are they *teenagers* or *younger*?

Do you like the music they listen to?

YES → Unless it's 80s rock, no self-respecting parent likes their teenagers' music! Put yourself on time out and send them with someone else.

NO ↓

Do you trust them?

NO → Of course you don't— they are teenagers!

YES → They are teens with hormones. They can't be trusted. Grab earplugs. You're chaperoning!

Is it a concert for kids?

YES → Are you willing to put yourself through that for their happiness?

YES → You are a rare breed of parent. Enjoy the concert, or bring noise canceling headphones.

NO → Invite your brother or sister to the "concert" and bail last minute. Make them take the kids. They'll get good uncle or aunt points!

NO → Is it a concert kids should go to?

NO → Don't be that parent who takes their kid to a "smoke" filled concert with a bunch of drunk people to feel cool. You're better than that!

YES → Bust out your T-Swift shirt and fan girl out with your kid!

Should I have a YARd SaLe?

Is your home CLUTTERED with stuff?

yes

Do you have a storage unit full of things you haven't used in a year?

yes

Get rid of some stuff before you end up on an episode of Hoarders!

no

Are the things you have in excess of good quality?

yes

Yard Sale it up! Make some money!

no

C'mon. Donate or throw away. You'll be doing that anyway after no one buys your crap.

Sale away! While you're at it, bust out a lemonade stand and have your cute kid run it. Cha ching!

yes

Are you trying to sell off your family disguised as a "yard sale"?

no

I literally know nothing about you. Do what you want!

yes

Sounds like I'll be watching you on 20/20 soon. Get some help!

no

Are you desperate for money?

no

Are you bored?

yes

What's your secret? I've forgotten what boredom feels like.

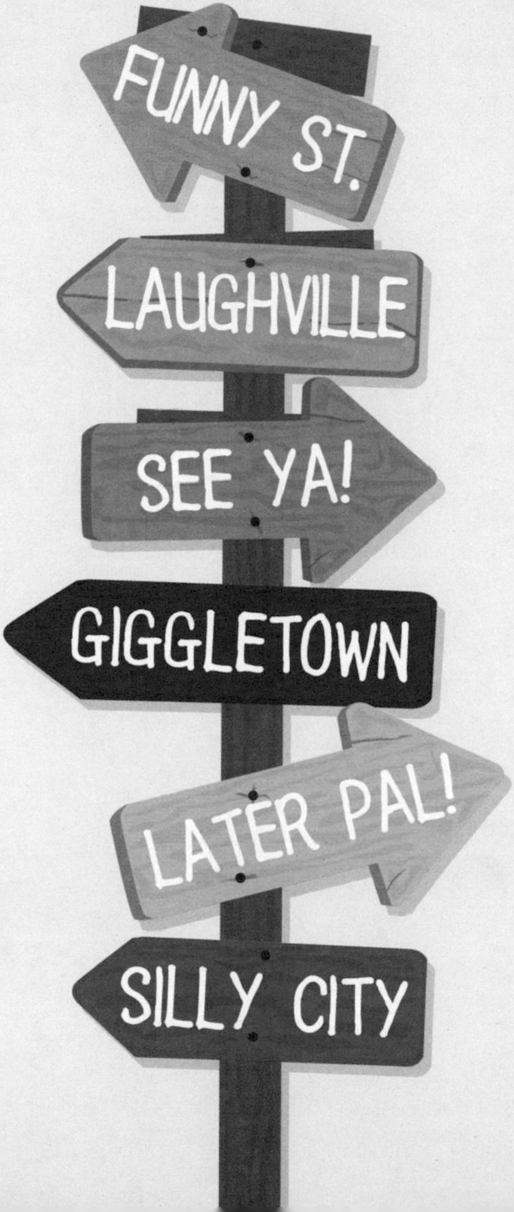
FUNNY ST.
LAUGHVILLE
SEE YA!
GIGGLETOWN
LATER PAL!
SILLY CITY

MOLLIE is a cosmetologist by trade and a comedian, public speaker, and trainer. She is also a wife and a mom of two teenagers. Mollie has been both a full-time parent and has worked outside the home during the different stages of her kids' lives. She has also been a little bit of a single parent during the times her husband, Heath, has had to travel a lot for work. This has given her all sorts of experience when it comes to different scenarios of raising kids, from the dirty diapers to the rotten attitudes and all the good stuff in between. She firmly believes there is not one way to parent and, in fact, doing everything "one way" is the absolute worst way. Through the triumphs and the complete disasters, moms need support and to know they are doing a good job. That's what this book is about—and a whole lot of silly nonsense. Enjoy and know your job matters.

ABOUT THE AUTHOR

HEATH HARMISON

Being a superhero was always an ultimate dream of Heath's . . . but due to his lack of athleticism, money, and tragic backstory, he decided that bringing laughter to the world would be the next best thing. He is a husband and father of two amazing kids, which is a great formula for great comedy. His observations of the struggles of fatherhood are hilarious and spot on. He's a full-time professional standup and improv comedian. His style of comedy kills in clubs, colleges, cruise ships, and festivals all over the world, including the Fringe Festival in Edinburgh, Scotland. In the last 13 years, Heath has performed and traveled to over 22 different countries. He's traveled overseas to perform for the U.S. Troops in Iraq, Kuwait, and Abu Dhabi and performs regularly on the Las Vegas Strip at Planet Hollywood, The Tropicana, and the MGM Grand! He has worked with some of the best comics in the business, including Brad Garrett, Louie Anderson, Dennis Miller, Eddie Griffin, and Roseanne Barr. His humor will burn images in your mind that will last weeks. For more laughs, visit Heath's website at www.heathharmison.com.

The End